T0085034

STEPHEN SONDHEIM
BROADWAY SOLOS

CONTENTS

THE CD IS PLAYABLE ON ANY CD PLAYER, AND IS ALSO ENHANCED SO MAC AND PC USERS CAN ADJUST THE RECORDING TO ANY TEMPO WITHOUT CHANGING THE PITCH.

ISBN 978-1-4234-7285-8

RILTING MUSIC, INC.

EXCLUSIVELY DISTRIBUTED BY

HAL•LEONARD®
CORPORATION

7777 W. BLUEMOUND RD. P.O. BOX 13819 MILWAUKEE, WI 53213

Visit Hal Leonard Online at
www.halleonard.com

ANYONE CAN WHISTLE
from ANYONE CAN WHISTLE

1/2

CELLO

Words and Music by
STEPHEN SONDHEIM

BEING ALIVE
from COMPANY

Music and Lyrics by
STEPHEN SONDHEIM

3/4

CELLO

BROADWAY BABY

from FOLLIES

CELLO

Music and Lyrics by
STEPHEN SONDHEIM

CHILDREN WILL LISTEN

from INTO THE WOODS

Words and Music by
STEPHEN SONDHEIM

CELLO

COMEDY TONIGHT

from A FUNNY THING HAPPENED ON THE WAY TO THE FORUM

CELLO

Words and Music by
STEPHEN SONDHEIM

GOOD THING GOING

from MERRILY WE ROLL ALONG

Words and Music by
STEPHEN SONDHEIM

CELLO

JOHANNA
from SWEENEY TODD

13/14

CELLO

Words and Music by
STEPHEN SONDHEIM

LOSING MY MIND

from FOLLIES

CELLO

Music and Lyrics by
STEPHEN SONDHEIM

NOT A DAY GOES BY

from MERRILY WE ROLL ALONG

CELLO

Words and Music by
STEPHEN SONDHEIM

NOT WHILE I'M AROUND

from SWEENEY TODD

Words and Music by
STEPHEN SONDHEIM

CELLO

OLD FRIENDS
from MERRILY WE ROLL ALONG

CELLO

Words and Music by
STEPHEN SONDHEIM

PRETTY WOMEN

from SWEENEY TODD

Words and Music by
STEPHEN SONDHEIM

CELLO

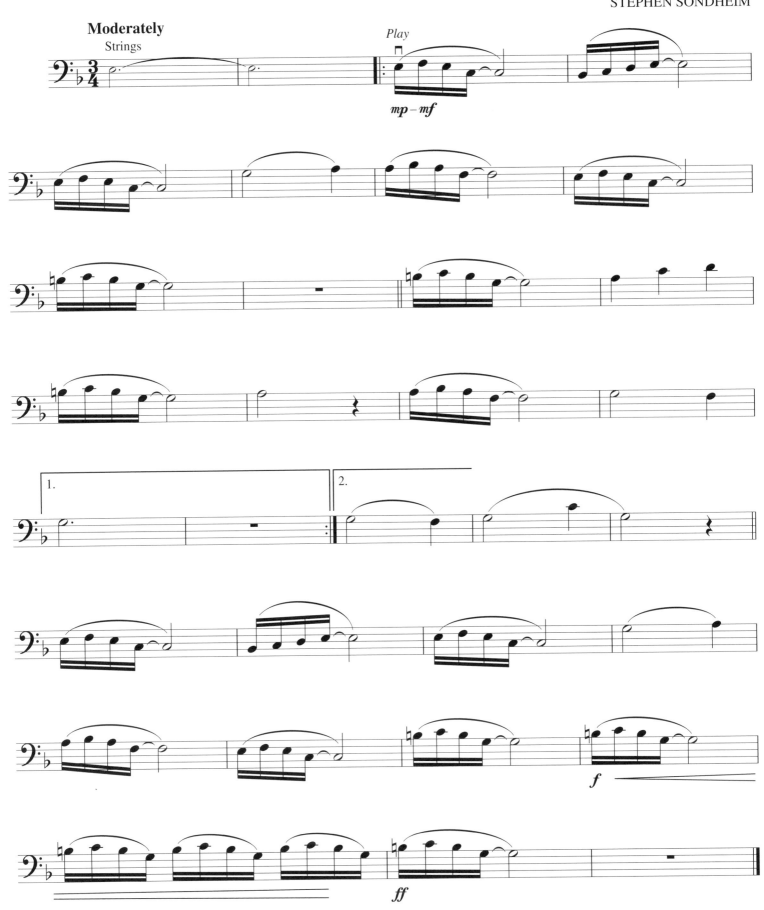

SEND IN THE CLOWNS
from the Musical A LITTLE NIGHT MUSIC

Words and Music by
STEPHEN SONDHEIM

CELLO

25/26

SUNDAY

from SUNDAY IN THE PARK WITH GEORGE

CELLO

Words and Music by
STEPHEN SONDHEIM